A Family Album

in Rhyme

Cotter Barry

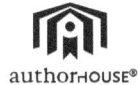

authorHOUSE®

AuthorHouse™
1663 Liberty Drive
Bloomington, IN 47403
www.authorhouse.com
Phone: 1-800-839-8640

First published by AuthorHouse   11/23/2011

ISBN: 978-1-4520-0636-9 (sc)
ISBN: 978-1-4685-2381-2 (hc)
ISBN: 978-1-4685-2400-0 (ebk)

Library of Congress Control Number: 2010904671

Printed in the United States of America
Bloomington, Indiana

This book is printed on acid-free paper.

Contents

Author's Foreword

As my family grew, so did my writing of poetry and prose. All have a special meaning for the most important areas of my life.

Over the years my wife began to share some of my writings with her friends and at their urging became "A Family Album in Rhyme"

I am sure you will find many of your life treasures in the reading of the treasures of my life in my family album. If so, you may want to read and re- read and share with your loved ones.

It is my hope that the reading of my family album will bring you the kind of spiritual comfort and joy it has given me in the creation of such. If my humble efforts help you or your loved ones to love and be loved, I will be more than amply rewarded.

COTTER BARRY

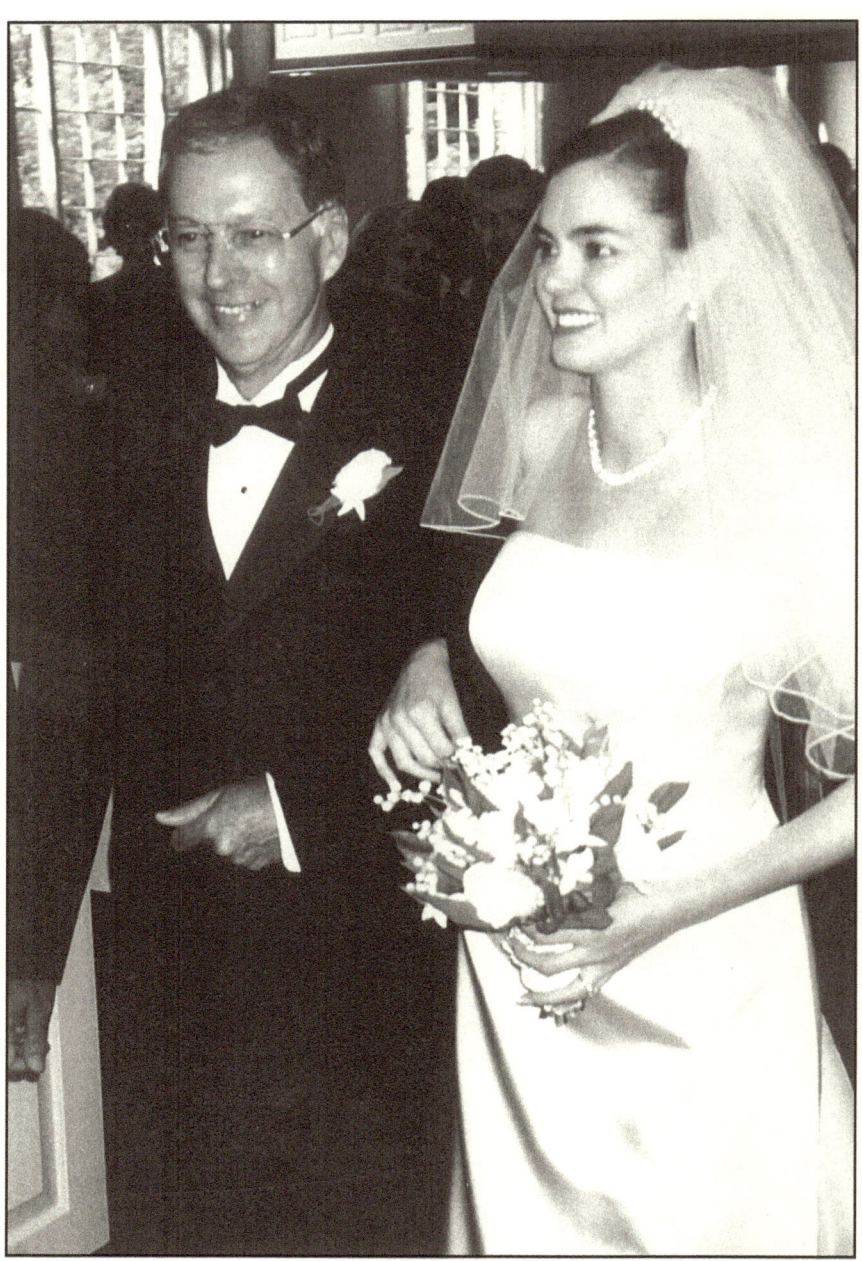

About the Author

Born and raised in a small coal mining town in northeastern Pennsylvania, Cotter Barry worked his way up the corporate ladder to ultimately become CEO of a Manhattan based insurance company In 1999, he retired from the corporate world to devote his time to his life long passion of writing. As a facilitator for workout sessions and retreats, Cotter Barry was known for addressing awkward subject matters and sensitive issues with a crafty folk style and a wordplay wit. As a poet and writer, his folk style evokes tears, laughter and anguish, as well as rekindles memories, Inspires courage and brings peace.

CHAPTER I

Family

· ·

Around the kitchen tables and within your family circles, the living substance of our nation is born, nourished and spread about our great country.

When I visit the place where I was born, I think of the care and love within my family circle and all the many experiences that had so much to do in making me who I am.

My earliest book was written within the hearts of my mother and father. No school, private club or social association has ever been able to furnish the warmth and understanding that my family gave to me.

The vital roots that nourished all that is good and worthwhile, in this world of ours, are exemplified in the family unit. Bitterness, hatred and jealousy have no place in a family.

The members of my original family remained together for a period all too brief. Separated from it my thoughts forever return. Then, when I took the plunge, I carried the world of my parents into the foundation of my new family circle. Of these I give to you…

A LOVING WIFE

We wish you
good health
joy
and special people
in your life.

We wish you
many wonderful
blessing
and the crowning
of a loving wife.

DAD'S DAY OFF

Dad planned to clean the garage today
    and store all the winter things away.

But a little boy called out a plea.
    Hey Dad, come play ball with me.

Dad put aside the work he planned to do
    and played with me till the day was through.

At bed time, I thanked him for playing ball
    and told him, he's the greatest dad of all.

He smiled and gave me a hug and a kiss
    then told me, no day will be as happy as this.

Cotter Barry

OUR OLD HOUSE

Our old house was not a castle,
    but I sure was happy living there.

Our old house gave many blessings
    and had so much love to share.

THANKS MOM

Thanks mom for teaching me the difference between right and wrong
and helping me to grow up safe and strong.

For not caring how long the road,
how tired you were, or how big the load.

Thanks for the hugs that eased my fears
and the kisses that took away my tears.

For helping me to settle down, start life's climb
by taking it one step-at-a-time.

For teaching me to hold my head up high
and hold fast to dreams, so they don't die.

For darning socks, turning collars and my first tie.
For baking all those cookies and my favorite huckleberry pie.

But for most of all, thank you for taking care of your little boy
and filling my heart full of love and joy.

Cotter Barry

MATER

Mater told me
waste not want not,
so I eat everything
she puts in my pot.

Mater punishes me
when I am bad.
Gives lots of hugs and kisses
when I am sad.

It's just mind over matter
so they say,
so pay attention to Mater
then go out and play.

I must say good-bye now
It's time to go
Not that I want, but
because Mater said so.

FATHER'S DAY

He turned me to the sunshine
    and encouraged me to dream,
Fostering and nurturing
    the seeds of self- esteem.

And when the winds and storms came,
    he protected me just enough.
Yet, not too much, for he knew someday
    I had to stand up and be tough.

His constant good examples always
    taught me right from wrong
Placing markers for my pathway
    that will last a lifetime long.

I am my father's son
    I am his legacy.
I hope today he feels his love
    reflecting back from me.

Cotter Barry

A LETTER TO DAD

There are many things
I like to tell you, face to face.
It's too late now for
I failed to find the time and place.

So in this special letter,
I'll try to express, at least in part,
The feelings that your passing
have left within my heart.

The memories of childhood days
and all that you have done,
To make our home a happy place
and growing up so much fun!

The memories of those walks we took,
the golf games we played.
Those confidential chats we had
while resting in the shade.

Thanks Dad for making my world a better place
and through the coming years,
I'll keep these memories of you
as cherished souvenirs.

SISTER

Because we were siblings and grew up together
    we shared certain bits of information.
That no one else on the planet knew
    that gave us a unique connection.

Like the time we hid behind the house
    to smoke our first cigarette.
And those old family jokes
    that outsiders would never get.

Trading mom's lunch with kids
    sitting in the back of the bus.
Those were the kinds of things
    that help make us, us.

Somewhere along the way, we became
    pretty good friends, you and me.
And in my opinion, that's just about
    as good as being family can be.

A WIFE

A wife,
I do profess
if you're so blessed,
is nothing less
than God's remedy
for loneliness.

MY MATE

My guiding light,
　　be that as it may,
understands what
　　I did not say.

The one still there when
　　everyone else is gone
the one and only
　　I fall back on.

Who was there for me
　　when I stumbled and fell
with encouragement and comfort
　　that all is well.

Forgiving when all others
　　are forsaking
never faltering even though
　　heart is breaking.

Cotter Barry

A BLESSING

May you feel whatever
    the air may bring.
Go places, take chances
    and have a fling.

Climb mountains, watch sunsets,
    hear birds sing.
Ride merry-go-rounds, go barefoot
    smell flowers in Spring.

So on this first day
    as husband and wife
We wish you happiness
    the rest of your life.

SON

You were unique right from the start.
At first sighting, you stole our heart.

Your zest for life has taken us far.
We asked for crumbs and got caviar.

No copies, no carbon, no clone
A uniqueness that's yours alone.

Incomparable among all on earth
With you we got our money's worth.

DAD TO DAD

Son, today you have someone to laugh yourself silly with,
    and to catch lightning bugs,
To giggle under the covers, receive butterfly kisses
    and Velcro hugs.

You now have a partner for blowing bubbles, flying kites,
    building sand castles and dancing in the pouring rain.
You'll be a hero for coaxing a wad of gum out of her hair,
    removing a splinter and kissing away the pain.

A hero for coaching her team that never wins
    yet always get treated to ice cream.
For carving pumpkins, playing hide-and-seek
    believing in magic and sharing her hope and her dream.

You'll now have an excuse to read of Piglet and Pooh
    watch Saturday morning cartoons and go to Disney Land.
To witness the endless wonders over rocks, ants and clouds
    and the joy of warm cookies and the holding of a small hand.

You now have a front row seat to history in the making;
    the first step, the first word and the first time behind the wheel.
Not to mention the education in human sexuality with
    the first bra and the first date...that will be a big deal.

For now, frame rainbows, hearts, flowers and collect
    spray pained noodle art and hand prints set in clay.
You'll get more love than your heart can hold
    and a glimpse of God everyday.

EVE, ACCORDING TO ADAM

When God made the world
    with its mountains and seas,
Its rivers and valleys
    and flowers and trees.

He paused for a moment,
    after doing so much,
Then gently added
    one last loving touch.

He made my Eve
    with her warm cheerful way
To add special beauty
    and joy to my every day.

He made her thoughtful,
    trusting and giving.
He made her gentle and kind
    with a great love for living.

He knew that some day
    a small part of Heaven above.
Would always be found
    in my Eve's love.

Cotter Barry

NANA

I like to walk with Nana
    her steps are short like mine.

She never tells me to hurry up
    she always takes her time

We always stoop and look around
    for things to see.

I'm so glad God made Nana
    unrushed and young like me.

GRANDPA

Mom didn't think I knew
    that grandpa likes to have a chew.
But juice on his shoe
    was always the first clue.

Mom didn't think I knew
    that grandpa made home-brew.
But getting a little dipsy-doo
    was a sure sign of Kickapoo.

Mom didn't know;
    when he put me to bed
Grandpa always said,
    "I'll be chewing you"
then patted me on the head.

Cotter Barry

MANY HATS

Many hats have been worn throughout the years;
    Each with its own purpose, bringing joy and/or tears.

There were chauffeurs and teachers, providers, enforcers;
    Psychologists, counselors, listeners, and supporters.

You've been coaches and spectators, sometimes referees;
    You've help mend broken hearts, and even scraped knees.

Each challenge accepted, no question asked.
    Not knowing the basis, of future tasks.

But two hats above all, you wear with such pride.
    "Mother" and "Father", with which you guide

And teach us the joy of unconditional love,
    that can only be surpassed by almighty above.

So thank you once more, for all that you do.
    But one more favor to ask, of both of you.

Two more hats to try on if it isn't a bother.
    Those being Grandmother, and of course, Grandfather!

W.C. Barry*

*The author of many hats is my son. This poem was given to his mother
and me the night we were told his wife was expecting their first child.
    The baton has been passed.

DOG TALK

Wags his tail when he is glad.
    Whimpers when he is sad.

Howls at the moon just like a wolf.
    To get attention, goes "woof".

To wake me from my nap,
    my face he will lap.

He's always talking to me
    even when he's scratching a flea.

Cotter Barry

CHAPTER II

Love

· ·

Love is both too easy to say and too hard to say. It can mean almost nothing to some and absolutely everything to most.

She loves her sister, he loves his car. She loves her husband, he loves his buddies, "love ya man". She loves her home, he loves the natural world around him. She loves her cat. He loves his dog. She loves her new shoes. He loves food.

Love never looks or acts the same. It is as different as the people who feel it. It is as different as you and I are different, yet it is there infusing all of life. Just one small world, encompassing everything. Love is the only sane and satisfying answer to our existence.

Sometimes love grows slowly unfolding over years. Sometimes it arrives out of the blue, full blown, complete and satisfying right from the get-go. Oh yes, it was love at first sight. For the lucky ones, it will stay that way forever.

Love is friendship, marriage and parenthood. Yet too many of us numb ourselves to the emotion of our daily existence. Many of us return a business call before the call from an old friend. We make sure we have eye contact when shaking the hand of a client, but on a day- to- day basis, barely look at our spouse. We take the time and listen to the needs of our coworkers over lunch and later that evening tune into the TV rather than our own children.

I'm certainly not an expert on this subject, however, BG and I just celebrated our 44th year as husband and wife, which in Hollywood years is about 120. You would think somewhere in between our first year and our forty fourth, I must have learned a few things. Perhaps, I'll let you be the judge.

FIRST SIGHT

She entered the room
    with a kindly air
and swept back from her neck,
    her tumbling hair.

When they saw her
    they broke out in song.
I'm delighted to say
    the naysayers were wrong.

MY SWAN

Love is
    romance, passion,
    desire and tenderness.

Love is
    honesty, candor,
    patience and gentleness.

Love is
    laxity, tolerance,
    devotion and forgiveness.

Love is
    giving, yielding,
    generosity and kindness.

Love is
    laughter, kisses,
    hugs and happiness.

Love is my swan
    of whom I've been blessed.

OLIVE

My new girlfriend
    is a dream come true

I like the way she wears
    her hair, and that curlicue.

She dresses like she just came
    from Saks Fifth Avenue.

And so smart, she's at the top
    of her class at Purdue.

Last night, she gave to me
    a big fat smackeroo.

Tonight, I'm going to tell her
    "olive you".

Cotter Barry

LOVE BEARS

I know Bears are very important
    for the Bible tells me so.
When I read the scripture
    I could tell from the after glow.

So pass it on to your offsprings,
    Hopes all things.
Believe in the Holly Scripture
    Love bears all things.

INSOMNIA

Insomnia is a contagious disease
    often transmitted by one's mate.
Honey, are you awake? I just can't
    sleep and it is getting late.

I got to address invitations, order
    the food and floral arranging need designed.
The reason you can't sleep is because
    you have too much on your mind.

The solution is easy.
    I'll tell you what I'll do.
I'll finish the invitations, order food
    and flowers, just for you.

As I laid there wondering
    how the promises I'm going to keep.
I looked over at my partner
    and found her sound asleep.

Why did I ever get myself
    in such a bind?
For now I can't sleep because
    I got too much on my mind.

MY LOVE

You are the wish
    I made upon a star

You are the moonbeam
    I carried home in a jar.

You are the one
    I always go to.

Because of you
    my dreams came true.

SLEEP

If you want to be
    at your very best
It's important you get
    a good night's rest.

If you want to have
    a sleep so sweet
Check yourself into
    a hotel suite.

If you want to be able
    to pull one's own weight
Your body and mind
    needs to recuperate.

If you want to keep
    your head on straight
Sleep only in a bed
    shared by your soul mate.

HEARTS AFIRE

Joy is the sound of words
    when the right one speaks them

Delight is the sound of songs
    when the right singer sings them.

Beauty awakes within
    when the sunset embers

Love lingers and sings
    and the swan remembers

A LONG TIME AGO

There was this little school
    on the side of a hill
And a pretty little girl
    that I remember still

MUSIC OF THE SOUL

A certain song
    brings an onslaught,
touching feelings
    words can not.

Down memory lane
    you take a stroll
to find the tie
    which bounds one's soul.

GONE

I viewed it with sadness
   but why should I sigh

She went off and married
   a real nice guy

IT MUST BE LOVE

If you feel it within
    it's time to give in.

if you hear it inside
    it's cupid by a landslide.

If you're glassy-eyed
    here comes the bride.

If she's a treasure trove
    it must be love.

FLOWERS OF EVERLASTING

A crown of moonbeams,
    stardust in her eyes,
Committed to love
    and family ties.

Her hand in his,
    a long time ago,
she told him
    she loved him so.

Timeless memories
    of those yesterdays
A part of the love
    we share in our today's.

Oh, how we've grown
    through dreams and sorrows.
A beautiful background
    for all our tomorrows.

Thank you for all
    the years we shared,
The ways you showed
    how much you cared.

To the years to come,
    as well as those of passing.
You are and always will be
    my flower of everlasting.

ON YOUR BIRTHDAY

As we celebrate the day of your birth
    we wish for you...
Gentle hugs to take away your hurt.

Friendship to brighten your being.
    Beauty for your eyes a seeing.

Rainbows to give you a fresh start.
    Sunsets to warm your heart.

Smiles when sadness intrudes.
    Laughter to accept poo-poo-pee-dooeds.

Songbirds singing high in a tree.
    Faith so that you can be free.

To march to your drum and fife.
    And love to complete your life.

FREE SPIRIT

A breath of fresh air, a voice divine,
    the warmth of her touch, a bit of angel- shine.

When asked to carry a heavy load
    took love to travel the lonely road.

A transforming touch sent light into gloom
    nameless magic put cheer in the room.

A smile in her voice, a song on her lip,
    a passion for life she did nip.

Pure in heart, she will always be
    self-respecting, a spirit that's free.

Cotter Barry

FROM THE HEART

Once again into your soul
you start to tip toe

To find the heart has reasons
which reason does not know

HAPPINESS

Happiness isn't for a chosen few
    you'll find it, in all that you do.

Collecting fireflies in jars
    under the evening stars.

Taking a ling walk in your favorite park.
    A cozy camp fire glowing in the dark.

A contended cat purring on your lap.
    Taking an after dinner nap.

Building castles in the sand.
    Taking a trip to Disneyland.

Holding hands with your wife
    to whom you've pledged your life.

Cotter Barry

NO REGRETS

It seems like only yesterday
    we stood side by side
And heard the words
    that gave to me a bride.

Though the years have swiftly flown
    and I have become silver gray
You've remained the same joy of my life
    as on our wedding day.

We traveled far, you and I
    drank from the sweet and bitter cups.
Rode the high roads and the downs
    but had fewer downs than the ups.

Through it all
    no matter where we roam
It's your smile
    that makes home sweet home.

Today, I say to the one
    standing by my side
I'd never regret the words
    that made you my blushing bride.

Chapter III

Children

•••••••••••••••••••••••••••••••••••

Having kids is an elastic concept for both Mom and Dad as well as their kid(s). Their kid's childhood will be fashioned by them collectively or individually in the case of single parent, fostered by society and their teacher(s), mined by the marketplace, especially TV, and protected by our own government. Well, occasionally and then only for some.

Today's kids, to me, are both brilliant and stupid. They are more culturally sophisticated, especially about consumption, yet profoundly naïve about responsibility. They text at the speed of sound yet can't write a simple thank you note. They are growing up too fast and, then again, too slow.

In the end, the advice will remain the same. Spend more time with your children. Be patient! Listen! Hold your breath and try to get through adolescence. You can worry. And then you can worry some more. It won't work as well as spending time with them and listening.

Children have never been very good at listening to their parents, but they have never failed to imitate them. Stay alert, be watchful and listen very carefully. When it is your turn to talk, and make sure it is your turn, level with your kid by being honest. Nobody spots a phony quicker than a child.

So what should we give our children?

WHAT SHOULD WE GIVE
OUR CHILDREN

Give them a sense of humor
    a place in the scheme of grinning
The passion of truth
    is a good beginning.

The knowledge of being loved
    and the awareness of these:
Songbirds, butterflies, rainbows
    and leafy trees.

The open sky, the brown earth,
    blue water and golden sand.
The beacon of hope
    reaching for a small hand.

Give them long days to be merry
    and nights without fear.
Unexpected kisses
    and a good home atmosphere.

Give them the will to work,
    the pulling of one's weight.
Give them your attention
    before it's too late.

Cotter Barry

A LITTLE PRAISE

Demanding perfection
    from a child
        is fiddlesticks.

For children have more
    needs of models
        than of critics.

Examples and merits
    are far better
        ways to raise.

For nothing has better
    effect upon children
        than a little praise.

TREAT OTHERS WELL

It is good that you
    teach you child how to
        read, write and spell.

But don't forget
    the value of friendship
        and treating others well.

BE KIND

Experience generosity,
go ahead and
upset the applecart.

Beyond what you think
are the limits to
expanding your heart.

Stretch the boundaries.
What you can do
is anybody's guess.

Be kind and generous
to the elderly.
They deserve your goodness.

PATIENCE

We need to be patient
    with our children
        and let them dream on.

Have patience like
    a tube of toothpaste.
        it's never quite gone.

SMILE

Cherish life,
yours
and others' style.

Do not
underestimate
the power of a smile.

Be cheerful
and friendly
every once in a while.

Why not
take a chance
and crack a smile.

CONFIDENCE

I know this will not come
　　as a big surprise,
Sometimes troubles are
　　blessing in disguise.

So stand up for yourself
　　no matter what the odds.
Give them lots of smiles
　　and a few confident nods.

WHAT'S WRONG

It's not wrong because
    "everyone is doing it"
    is not acceptable.

It's not wrong because
    "they told me to do it"
    is not being accountable.

It's not wrong if
    it's good for us
    is not top drawer.

It's only wrong if
    I get caught
    is not my mentor.

To know it's wrong
    doesn't make you
    a dinosaur.

What's really wrong is
    nobody seems to know
    what's wrong anymore.

Let's remind them.

TODAY'S PEACOCK

Be humble enough to admit
    someone else is crème de la crème
and wise enough to learn
    how to work to surpass them.

Be smart enough to recognize
    everyone can not run the show
and that a peacock today
    may be a feather duster tomorrow.

Cotter Barry

EXPRESSION

Before you decide
    on having a tattoo

And placing such
    for the world to view

Or when you wear white
    it'll show through.

You might want to consider,
    just consider, mind you

An expression of feeling
    can take another avenue.

FOR SALE

Selling your brain,
     if you so incline,
is just taking advantage
     of a gold mind.

Sell your brains,
     put yourself on the payroll.
But never put a price
     on your heart and soul.

TWO EVILS

If you find yourself
    in the midst of upheavals
And you must choose
    between two evils

Don't pick the one
    you abhor.
Pick the one
    you have never tried before.

ILLUMINATION

Pass on the light
    within us brothers

To illuminate
    that within others.

TOO BUSY

When you are too busy
   for your friends
      you are too busy.

TODAY

It's over and can't be changed
    so don't regret yesterday.
Enjoy the day God gave you,
    enjoy the moment, enjoy today.

Don't worry about tomorrow
    because when it gets here,
It usually isn't as bad
    as you thought it would appear.

When tomorrow becomes today
    everything will be okay.
Enjoy the day God gave you.
    enjoy the moment, enjoy today.

Cotter Barry

LETTERS FROM THE HEART

Grumble if you must
    but wouldn't it be better
To paint a picture
    or write a letter.

To bake a cake
    or plant a seed
Ponder the difference
    between want and need

Does it really matter?
    that so called
Corporate ladder.

There is so much to do
    and so little time
There are rivers to cross
    and mountains to climb.

Music to hear
    and books to read
Friends to cherish
    and life to lead

Cry if you want
    but the world's out there.
With the sun on you face
    and the wind in your hair.

A flutter of snow
    a shower of rain
This day will not
    come around again.

Fuss if you must
    but bear in mind
Old age will come
    and it's not kind

And when it's time
    for you to depart
You'll wish you wrote
    a letter from the heart.

Cotter Barry

COMMON SENSE

The sound judgment
    of mankind to decide
Which is wise to undertake
    and what should be set aside.

Nature's priceless gift,
    given so we can share.
It is as valuable as
    it's application is rare.

POISE

The man of resolve
    will never experience unpleasantry.

He knows exactly what he wants
    and what he can do.

Marching ahead steadily
    eyes fixed upon the goal.

Paying no heed whatsoever
    to misleading propose.

Which cripples his breath of soul
    depriving him essential energy

Vital in preserving
    his ever poise.

The power derived from
    the mastery of self.

Cotter Barry

WRITE RIGHT

Thank you for watching what your write,
for words are powerful and wonderful things.
They can be sweet as bees' fresh honey
or hurt like their terrible stings.

Like warm milk taken at night
they can comfort a lonely life.
But when written in anger, they can cut
like a sharp two −edged knife.

If a bitter revengeful spirit prompt
the words, keep them under seal.
For the wounds they make
are always slow to heal.

May your pen always characterize
truth and be kind.
Written to support the old and weary,
to comfort and help the blind.

Thanks for turning darkness into light,
your kind words and action of right.
For making my life most sweet and
for taking the time to write.

WORRY

Worrying is like
    sitting on grandpa's porch
        in a rocking chair.

It gives you
    something to do but
        doesn't get you anywhere.

FREE WILL

The power of human beings
    doctrines professes
That responsible choice
    everyone possesses

The good preacher told me
    it's time to rejoice
Believe in free will
    you have no choice

But dad told me
    son don't go astray
Man has his free will
    but woman has her way

CHAPTER IV

Folks

• •

When you're establishing a home, nothing beats having good neighbors. In this I have been most fortunate. It was not an unusual house, yet it drew me in with its welcome mat. The people who lived there were friendly to all who passed. They smiled and greeted me and gave themselves with mind and heart.

Do you know your neighbor and the people who live and work in your town? Do you ever take the time to talk a bit and listen to his troubles, his heartaches, his cares?

Do you bid your neighbors "good morning' and a greeting of "how do you do" or pass him by as if he was nothing to you?

It seems everyone is in a rush these days and don't have the time to visit awhile. The fact this fellow you're living beside is a guy just like you with a heart that will respond in kind if you just stop to give him a message of cheer.

Meet the folks who entered my life in a casual way and saw at a glance what I needed. There were others who passed yet not one of them heeded. Perhaps they were thinking of other folks or of themselves.

POET

The singer songs from the heart
    expressions in the mart

Children's faces, oh so sweet
    dew-wet grass beneath your feet

Singing birds and humming bees
    lighthouse shines and speaking trees

Snow top mountains
    bubbles forming in fountains

Sea gulls on upward wings
    of places and quiet things

Mighty rivers and bubbling streams
    youthful hopes and dreams

Tutorship from the passage of time
    reflection of life, put into rhyme

Cotter Barry

THE PLEADER

Sufficiently persuasive
    to present advantageously their case
The bearing of a person
    even more than his face.

Nothing is more disastrous
    than an idea inadequately defended
Unless it be a rightful claim
    that is inexactly presented.

TEACHER

He speaks of no one but you
    to you now the question he will take.

You are charged with a great responsibility
    the mind of my child you will make.

Complains you give him too much work
    yet studies hard.

Looking for your approval
    the whole nine yard(s).

Keep alive his desire for knowledge,
    instill in him a dream.

Encourage in him individualism
    as well as a player on a team.

To reason logically,
    aim high, the stars to strife.

To have an uncompromising conscience
    the foundation of life.

Cotter Barry

STABLEMAN'S DAUGHTER

She was mounted on a stallion
    equipped with a saddlebag.
I tried to start up a conversation
    as I sat on my nag.

She talked about mares, colts
    foals and fillies
Broncos, mustangs, hacks,
    trotters and ponies.

I was a tiller of the soil,
    of compost, dung and manure.
She was the stableman's daughter
    and all the "horse-men-knew-her".

IRRAITANT

A problem, a pain and stubborn as a mule,
    we thought of ourselves as the dynamic dual.

In the way, annoying, disruptive on her date,
    the world irritants, seemed to her appropriate.

Amusing, comical, two monkeys looking for a chuckle
    designed a scheme, a big sister would ruffle.

Pleasantry, dad said with laughter
    it's just two kids, acting like Katz and Jamer.

They irk, bother, provoke and provide amusement
    so tell your date you have built in entertainment.

Oh Father, that thought it utterly flagrant
    henceforth they shall be called "irritant".

Cotter Barry

MUSICIAN

I always wanted to be a musician;
to blow a horn or strum a guitar
join a band and travel far.

To sing Dixie and pluck a banjo
tickle a keyboard or a grand piano.

I always wanted to be a musician;
like Ringo Starr and beat a drum.
Clashing symbols seemed like fun.

Swinging the scales on saxophones
marching in the parade with 76 trombones.

I always wanted to be a musician;
to write a song that would be newsworthy
but found myself, not noteworthy.

CABINET MAKER

What's a cabinet maker
    you asked of me
Now let me think
    I know of three

Adviser of a sovereign
    and a head of state
One who makes fine furniture
    that holds a plate

On the other hand
    to UK's Parliament
A cabinet maker named Fanny Hill
    was a heavenly event.

Cotter Barry

THE WRITER

You will hear it inside
   you will feel it within

Awakening thoughts called fourth
   by the magic power of the pen

MATH PROFESSOR

Do you believe
    at JFK airport today
A public school teacher,
    wearing glasses and a toupee.

Was arrested for possession
    of a ruler and a protractor,
a set square
    and a calculator.

Believed to be a member
    of al-Gebra connection.
Is being charged for carrying
    weapons of math destruction.

BAKER'S WIFE

Although he made lots of dough
    he hungered for a young bride.
Among the biscuits and the rolls
    he found the fairest by his side.

Decorating cookies, baking cakes
    and home made apple pies,
A batter smeared angelic face
    looked into his craving eyes.

He saw a young beautiful flower
    about to blossom,
like the mythical yeast.
    She thought he was handsome.

If you knead to know
    the flour of his life
was only a baker's dozen
    when she became the baker's wife.

PACK RAT

If you are like most of us
    you have too much stuff.
So think about cleaning the house
    and bring things up to snuff.

Think of all the things you have
    that are gathering dust
and the things that have been around
    so long they are starting to rust.

Now think of the people
    who have it rough
and the difference it would have
    on those who do not have enough.

We are not asking to give it all away.
    for some stuff you can't leave.
But you should know it really
    is more blessed to give, than to receive.

Cotter Barry

BEST FRIENDS

Like two peas in a pod
    are Attie Belle and Bee Gee

From high school days
    when they were carefree

To the celebration of
    their golden jubilee

Through thick and thin
    they never disagree

And in the years to come
    it's a guarantee

The best of friends
    they will always be.

STORYTELLER

Although it was always
    a story done well.
It was always a story
    he could not tell.

For his voice was soft and
    gentle, yet quite deep.
When he talked it was
    like counting sheep.

When he looked at the lis'ners
    they were all asleep.
He slammed the book and
    to their feet they leap.

With the listeners
    he established a foothold.
and the story worth telling
    was finally told.

Cotter Barry

CRITIC

I can't do that, it will not work
    I've always been that way;
Limits perspective and
    is nothing more than self flay.

Self criticism, like swearing
    is just a bad habit.
It's something we get used to
    that drains our spirit.

It keeps us busy
    gives us something to embrace.
Common sense tells us
    you're not in the race.

Dismiss negative thoughts
    that fill your day.
A more peaceful feeling
    is only a moment away.

When you feel uptight
    cut yourself some slack.
Don't let the small stuff
    throw you off track.

Learn to take
    yourself less seriously
Go with the flow
    respond more peacefully.

In order to become
   more optimistic
Stop expecting things to go wrong
   and silence your critic.

BUTCHER BUTCH

Butch started his career
    as a deli worker.

It's a sad story to tell,
    a real tear-jerker.

Butch didn't cut the mustard,
    at times he was a dork.

He backed into the meat slicer
    and got a little behind in his work.

Photos

· ·

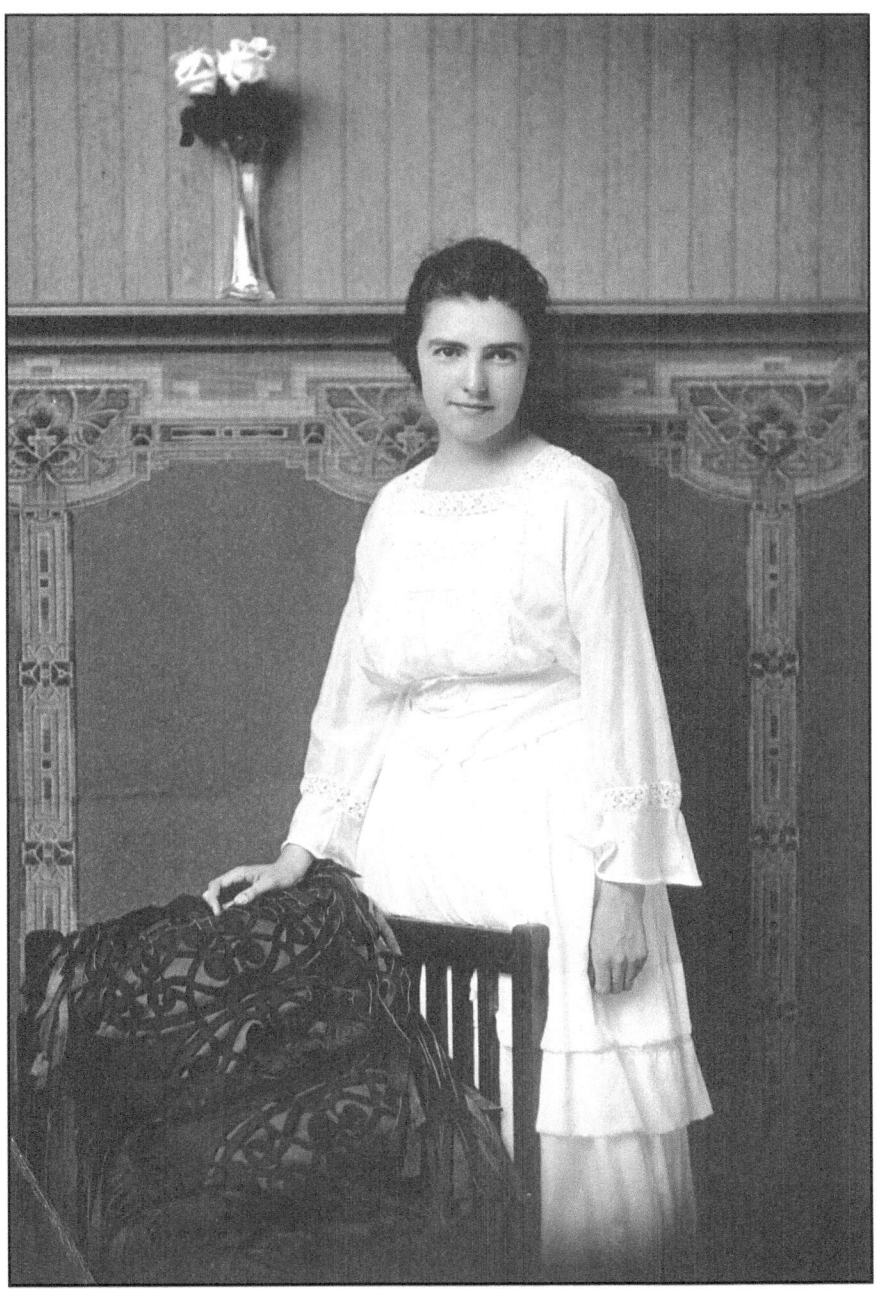

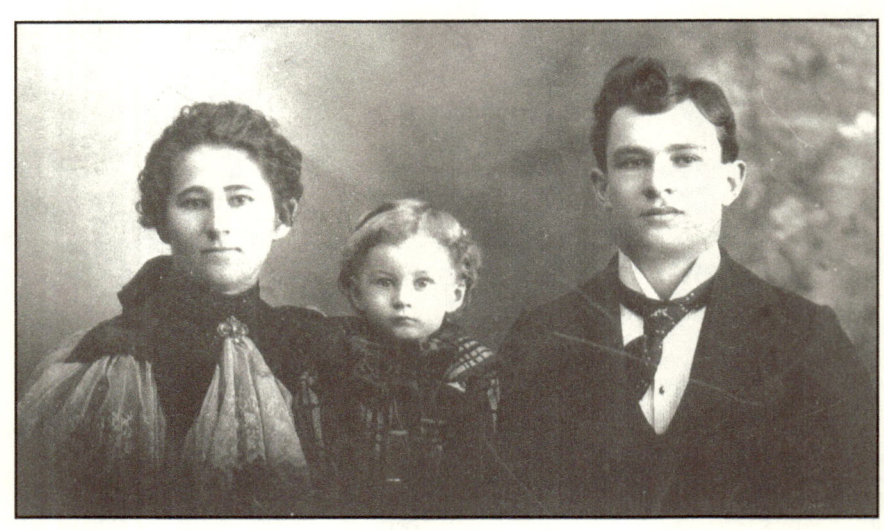

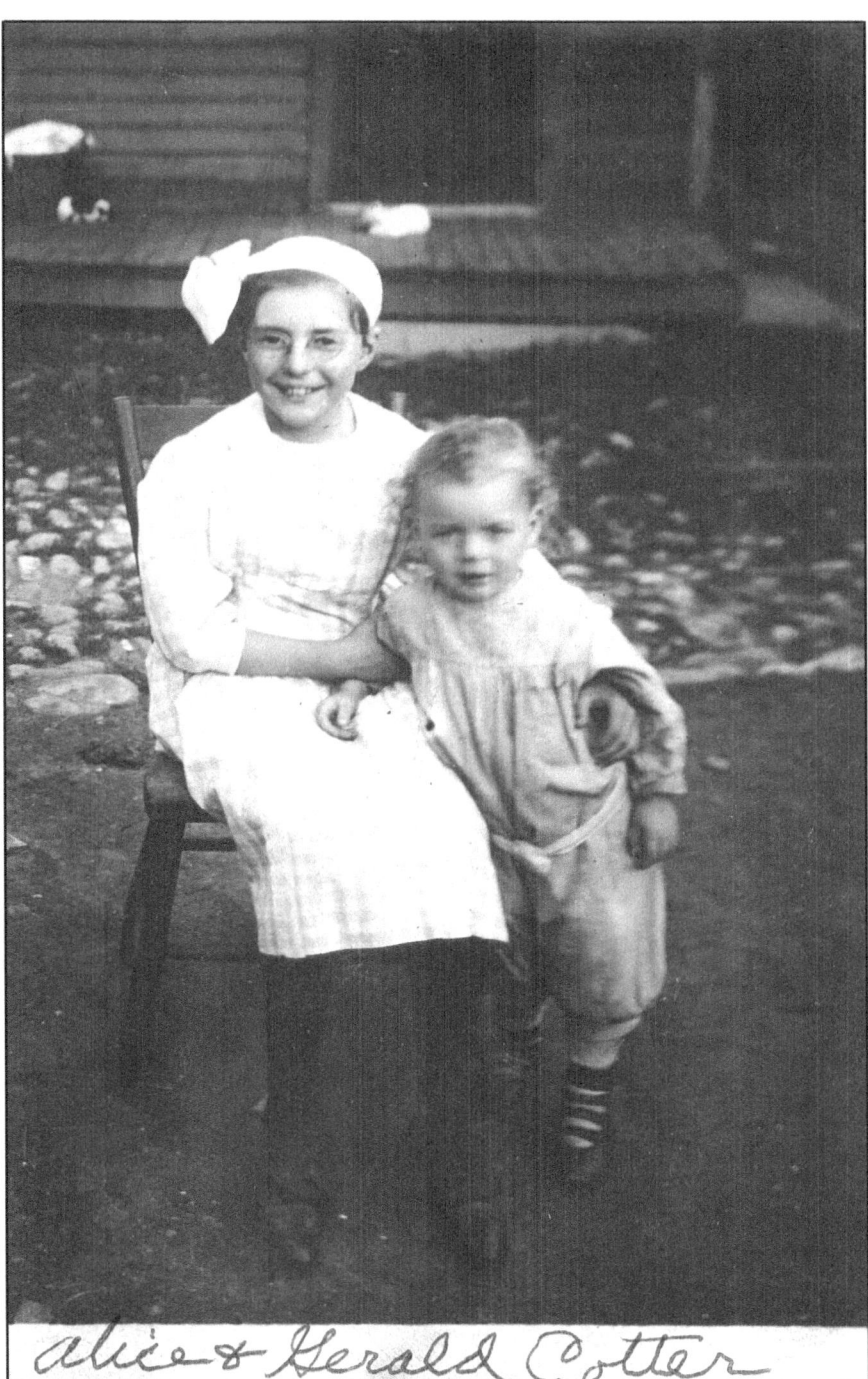

Alice & Gerald Cotter

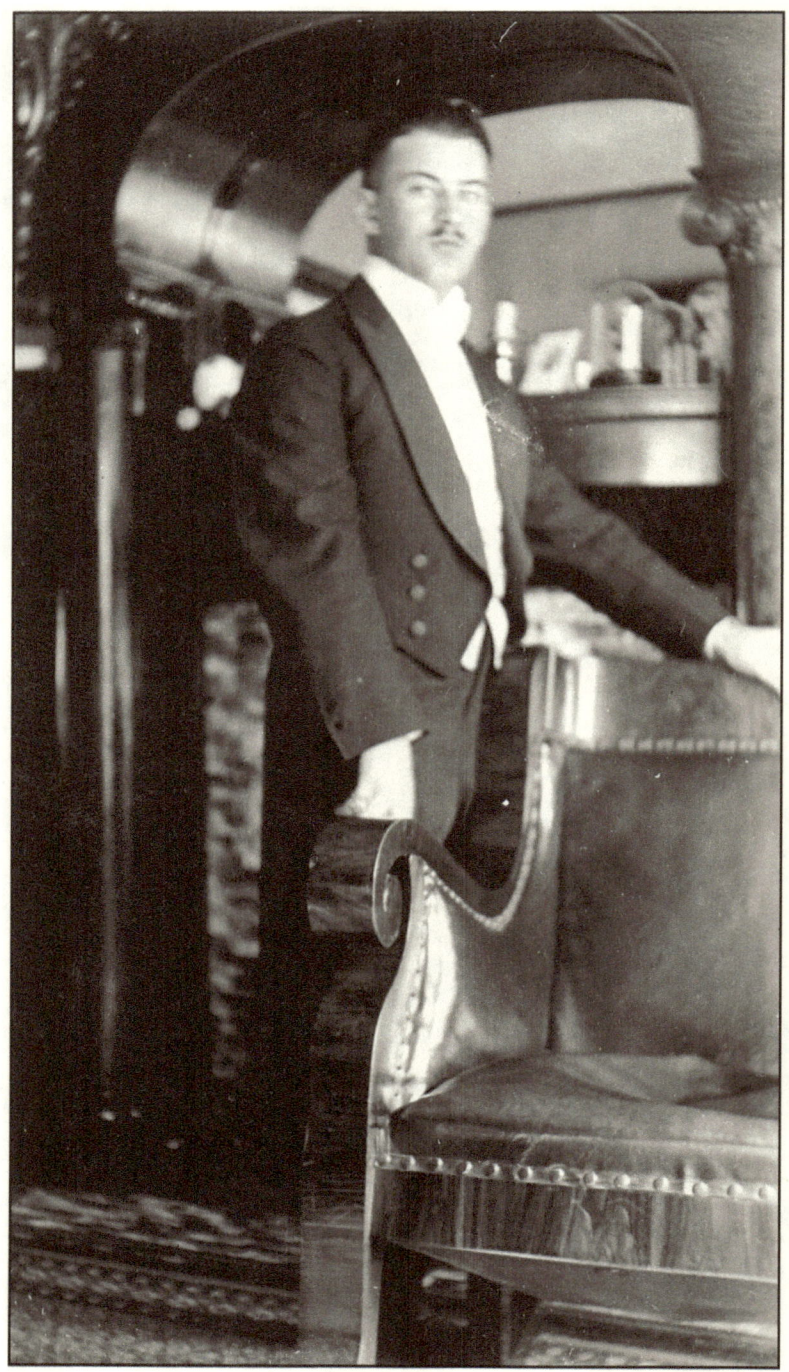

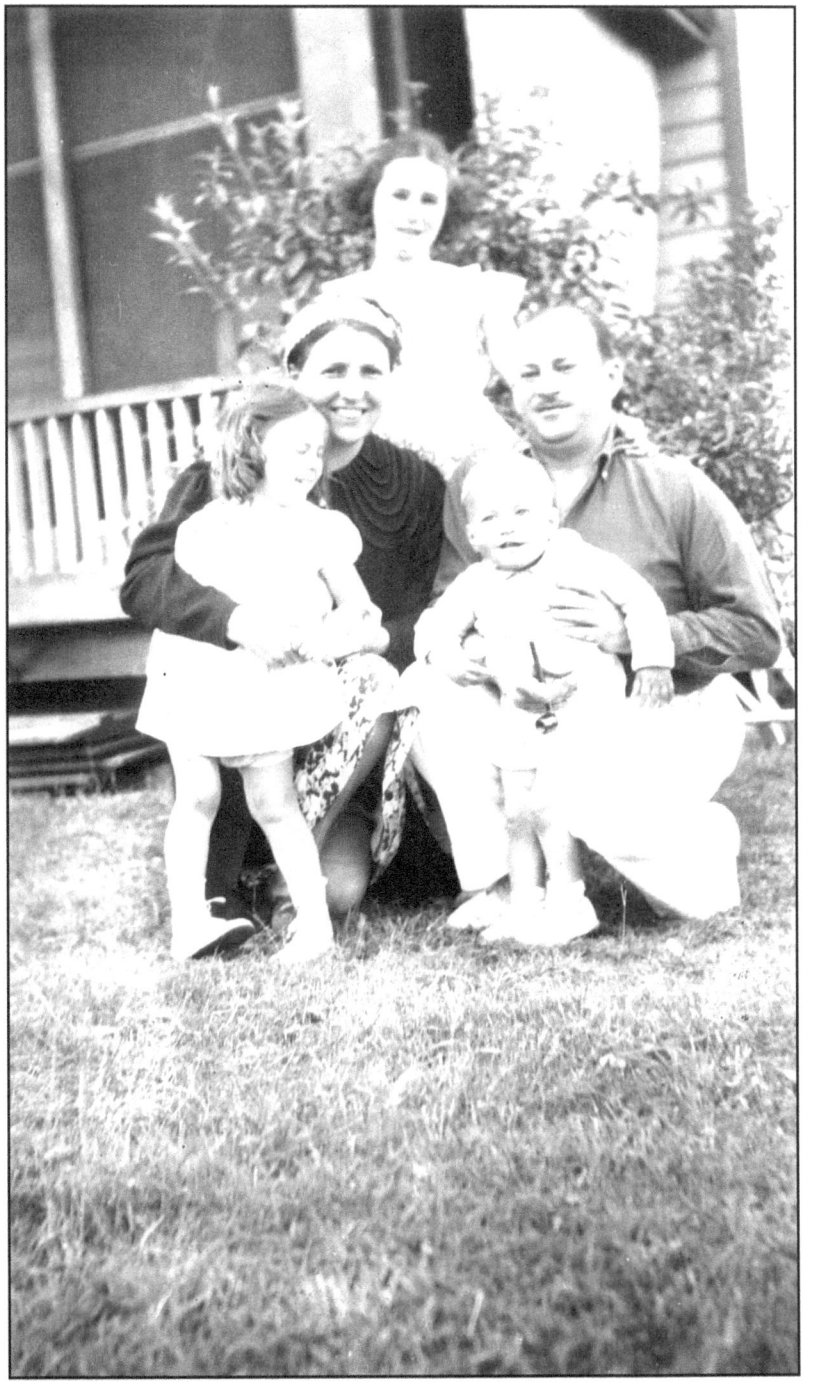

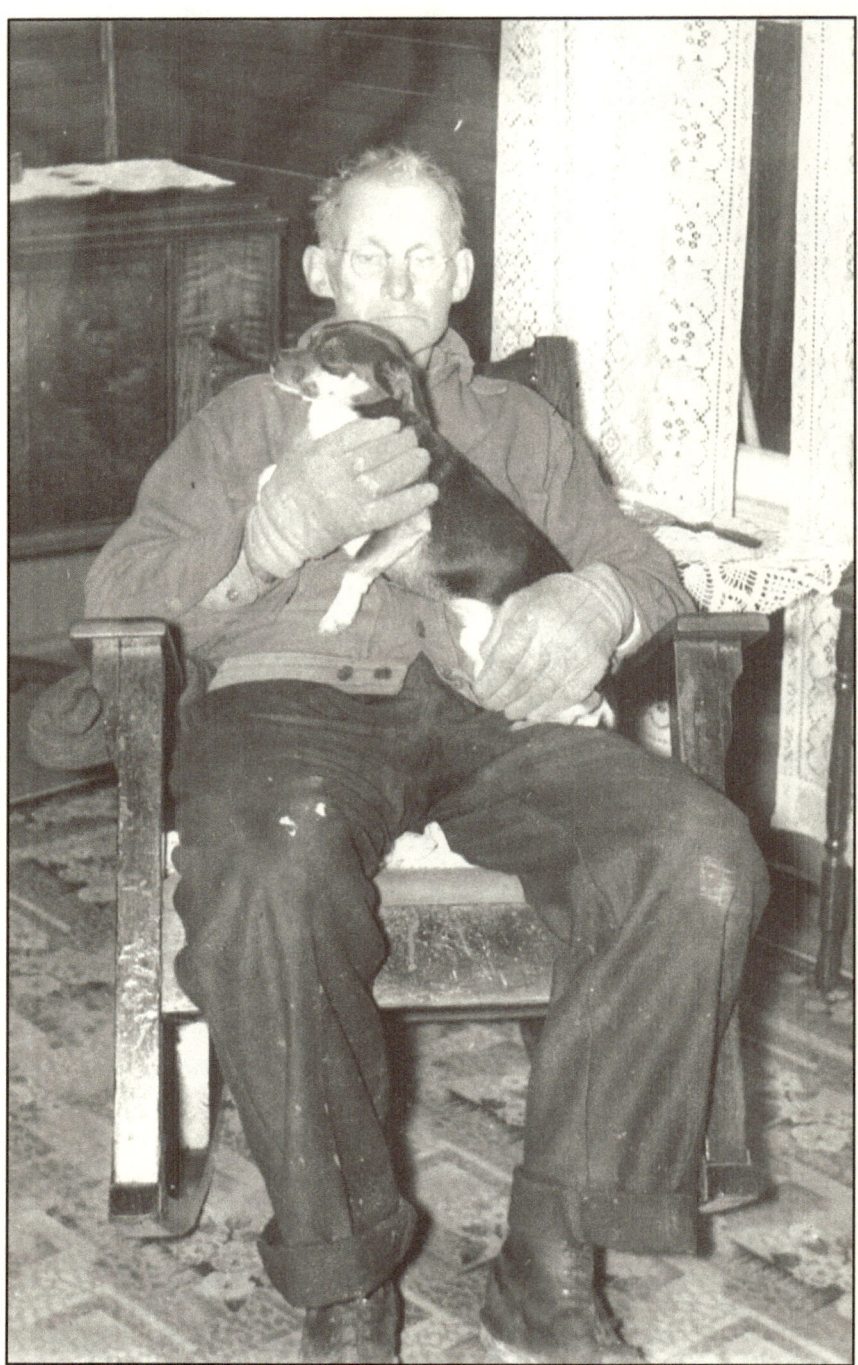

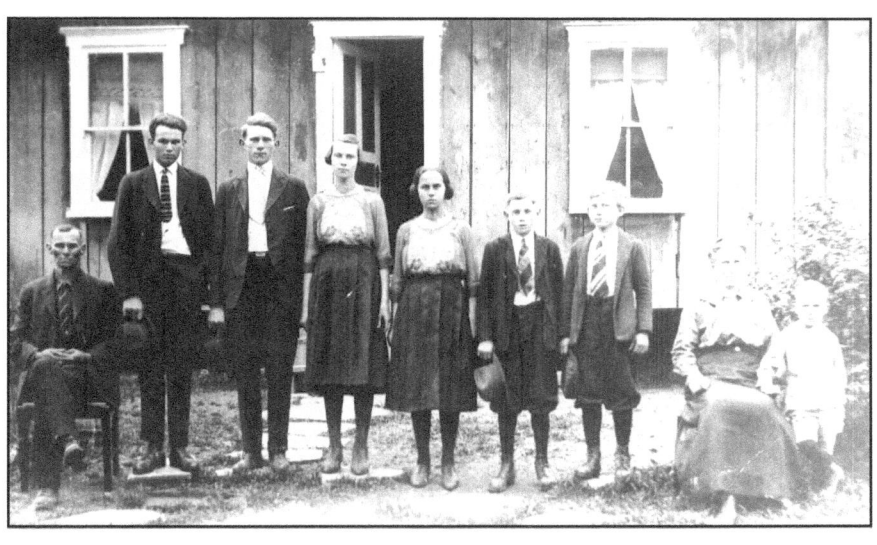

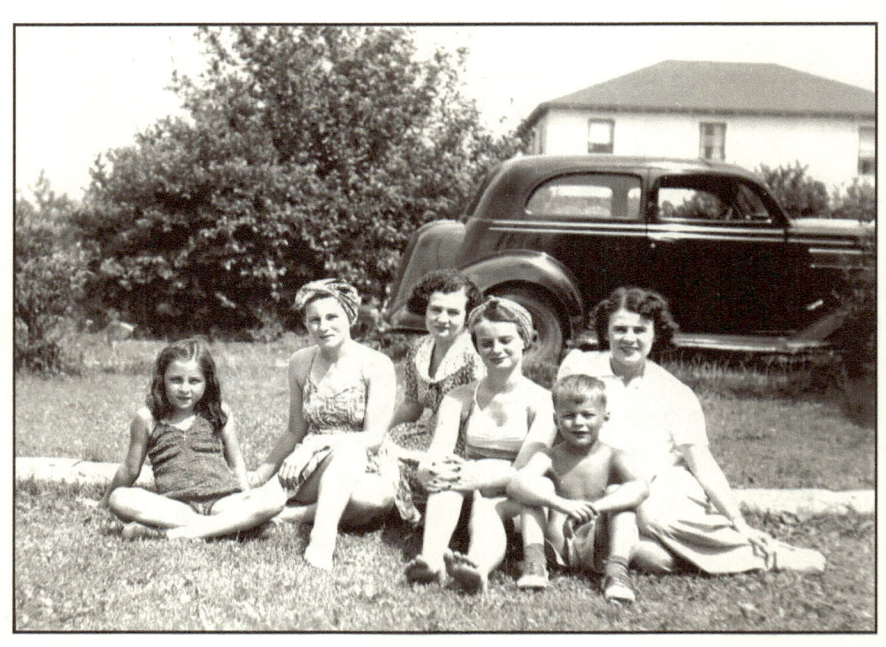

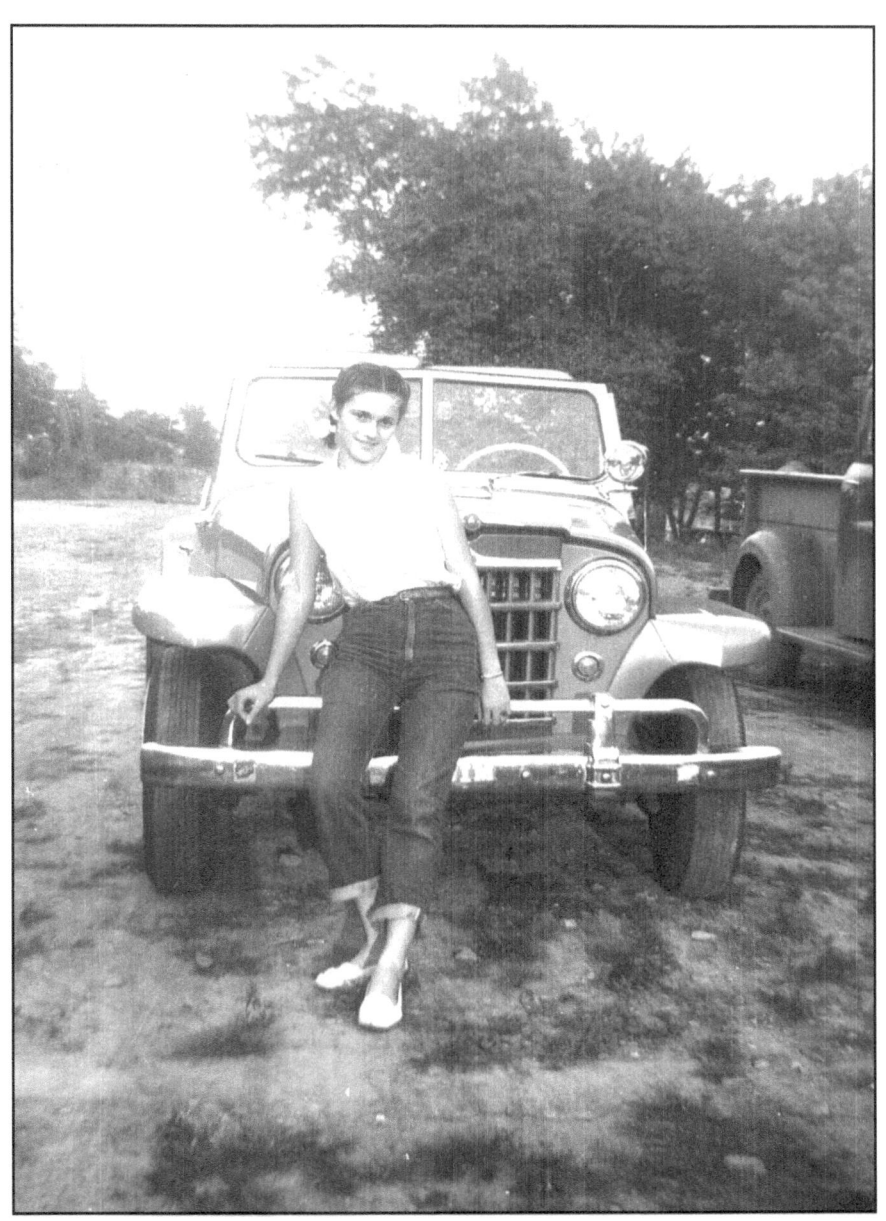

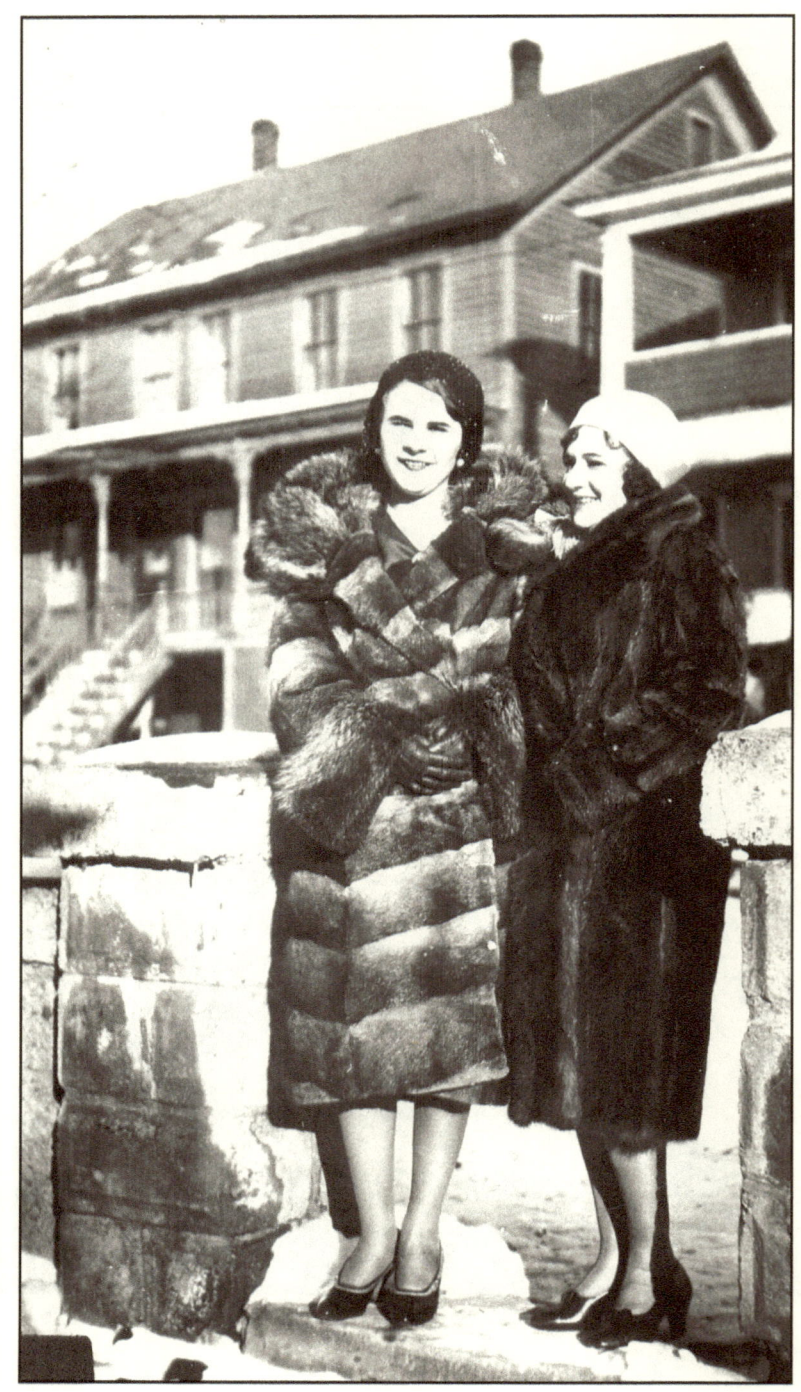

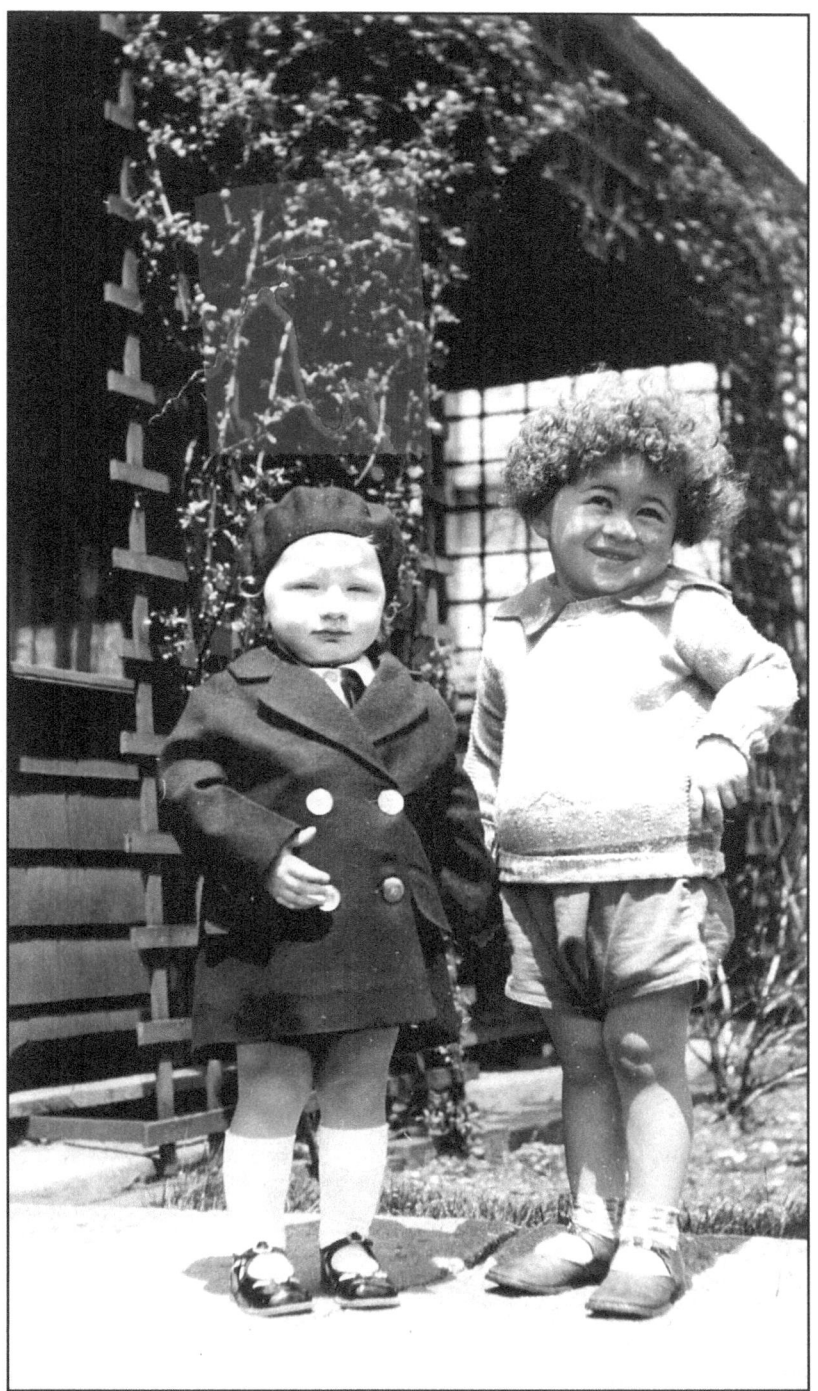

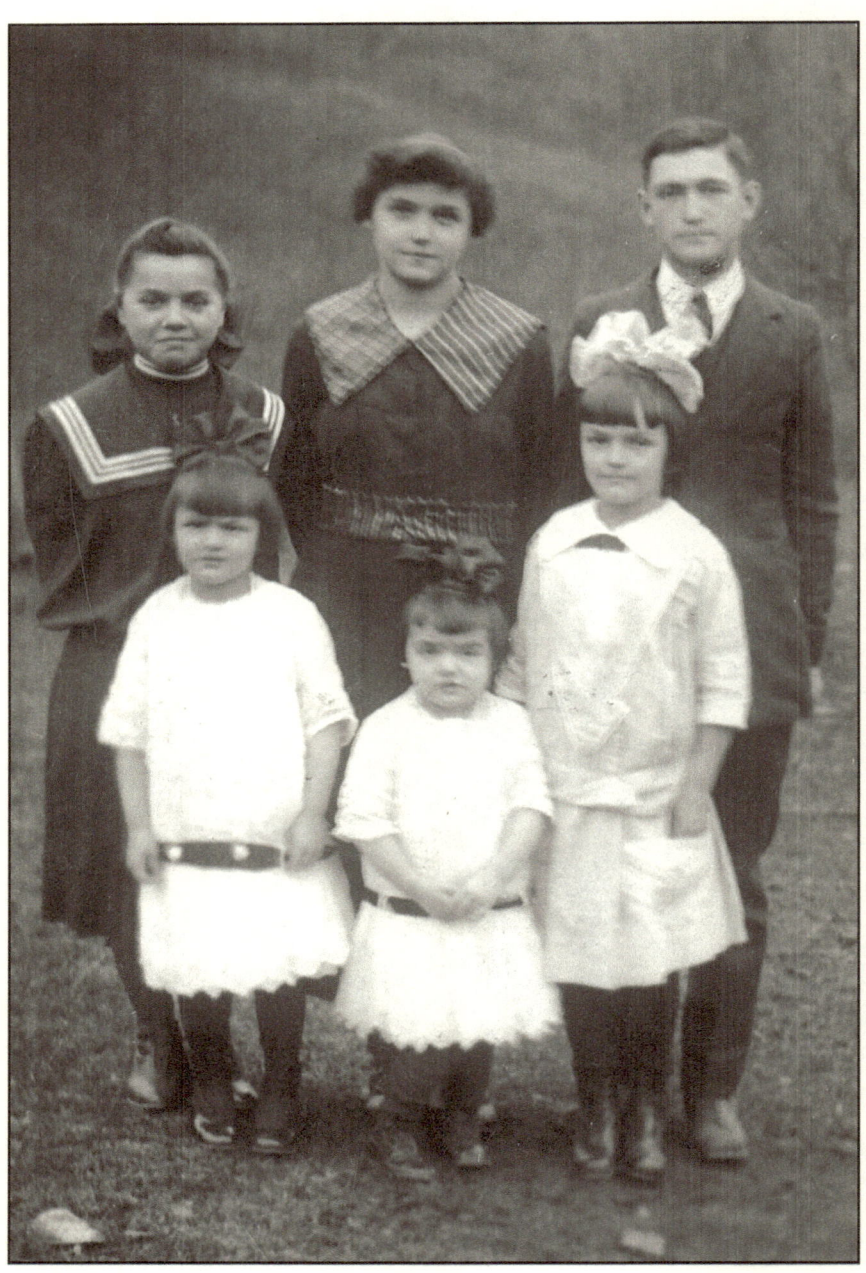

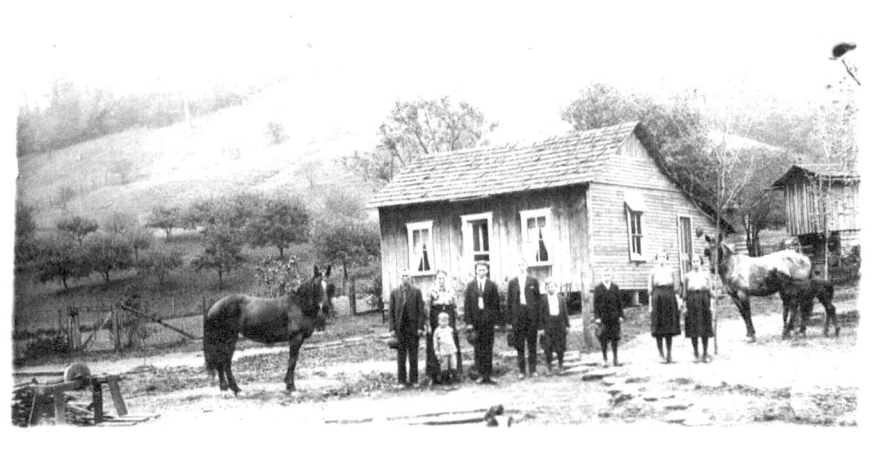

CHAPTER VI

This About That

· ·

As I recall our 37th President, Richard M. Nixon, favorite expression during press conferences was, "let me say this about that'.

"This" section is about "that" stuff that does not fit into anything special, yet I wanted to say this about that. Why not, if it is good enough for Tricky Dick, It's good enough for me.

In case you were wondering most people in Canada do not like us. When I go up north I spend most of my time listening to complaints about the USA and its policies. For example; the US does what it wants without regard to the consequences it may have in its friends to the north. My response was, "so what's your point?"

One thing that is troublesome to me about our political system is that it seems to scare off people who might have made great presidents and attacks those who...oh well, you can finish the sentence.

Did it ever occur to you, that failure to recognize roots and ignorance of history will lead to a decline in morality and spirituality. The moment we give up our principles and family values...The moment we laugh at those who hold dear those principles and those values, we die and become surface people.

You know the type of people I am talking about. The shallow people with the fake smiles and empty words, whose conversations centers around themselves. The one's with no depth. The one's without compassion, love and feeling for others. The ruthless one's without ruth, the heartless one's without heart and the dead one's without a soul.

Now that I got that off my chest, I would like to invite you to join me in fellowship and a "sip" with my discriminating fellow squires.

You are to be commended, where even you may be, for your considered prejudice in favor of limestone water and the leisurely patient ways of "the hollow."

May you always ride an easy- walker, sleep beneath a rain-tight roof and eat high on the hog every day of your life.

Now that we are joined spiritually and enjoying out "sip" let me say "this about that" in rhyme, for I feel less alone when I write poetry.

LESSONS LEARNED

I've learned
    that those who reach their goals to easily
    have aimed too low.
    If you want to draw a crowd
    pass out some dough.

I've learned
    that good or bad, most things
    don't last very long.
    However, bad things end up
    in a western song.

I've learned
    you never have insomnia
    when it's time to get up.
    Nothing starts in the morning
    until your first cup.

I've learned
    when corporations start losing money
    there is going to be an axing.
    And to a worm, going fishing
    isn't very relaxing.

I've learned
    that when you want a garment
    to shrink, it won't.
    Yet they come out of the dryer
    two sizes smaller, when you don't.

Cotter Barry

I've learned
    everyone wants to live
    on top of the mountain.
    To taste the waters of success
    you must go to the fountain.

HAPPINESS

To climb the corporate
    ladder to success
takes hard work
    and nothing less.

After all those years
    I must confess
It is time
    to discover happiness.

OUR TIME

We have greater success
but seem to enjoy less

The more we acquire degrees
the less we know our ABC's

The more medicine we profess
the less time we spend on wellness

The bigger the crime
the less we serve time

We have increased our revenues
but decreased our values

The more anger we display
the more seldom we pray

THE DAY AFTER

Did you ever notice that,
After the presents have been unwrapped
and Santa has been decapped

After the carols have all been sung
and stockings are no longer hung

After the food has all been eaten
and the hugs have all been given

The spirit of Christmas seems to disappear
rather than stay with us the rest of the year.

Cotter Barry

SELF CONTROL

When I was young
    I had no brains
        but a heavenly body.

Over the years
    I grew in wisdom
        and became squatty

For self control
    I will never be
        magna cum laude

RAINY SUNDAYS

Rainy Sundays are
        for quiet reading
If you are into gardening
        a time for weeding.

Rainy Sundays are
        for budget juggling.
Lighting the fireplace
        is great for snuggling.

Rainy Sundays are
        for friends and rapping.
Watching old movies
        or just plain napping.

Cotter Barry

HARD WORK

Good things
are within your reach
he uttered
with a gasp.

Do not forget
it takes hard work
to get them
in your grasp.

SUMMER STORM

The night is heavy
with heat and grime
As I hasten
to get home on time.

The thunder afar
is suddenly near.
The noise has me
trembling with fear.

The air is still
muggy with heat
The flashes of lightening
brought scurrying feet.

The storm winds moves
trees to and fro
Not tree by tree
but with one big blow.

In the morning I awake
to sweet freshness I gain.
As the sun dries clean
the puddles of rain.

TELLTALE

It really doesn't make any sense
    your effort to keep up false pretense

For I can tell who you are, by the friends you seek
    and the very manner in which you speak.

The way in which the corporate ladder you climb
    and the way you employ your leisure time.

I can tell who you are by the things you wear
    and the spirit in which your burdens bear.

By the manner in which you bear defeat
    and by simply watching how you eat.

I can tell what you are by the way you walk
    and the subjects in which you delight to talk.

By the books you choose from the library shelf,
    for all these ways and more, you tell on yourself.

FEAR

Venturing in the darkness
    and walking haphazardly
I found myself confronted by obstacles
    which I was unable to foresee.

Frightened by forms whose
    nature I can not define.
Silhouettes of assassins
    were really branches of a tree.

Cotter Barry

QUIET TIMES

I still have an hour
    before the phone begins to ring.
At least an hour before
    someone asked me to do something.

There is something peaceful
    about being alone
Having some time without
    the ringing of a phone.

Just ten minutes for meditation,
    a walk down nature's path
Locking the bathroom door
    and taking a long bath.

A quiet place where you let go
    instead of resisting with all your might
A place where life begins to flow
    a place you become less uptight

Alone on the beach walking
    barefooted in the sand.
Where relaxation and creativity
    go hand-in-hand

IT'S TIME

It's time to get, a time to lose.
A time to decide, a time to choose.

Whether to keep or to cast away,
A time to leave, a time to stay.

A time to look up, not down the track.
A time to go forward and not look back.

No more silence, it's time to say.
It's time for the coming of a new day.

It's time for laughter...no time to cry.
It's time to say the last good-bye.

Cotter Barry

A MIRACLE

You see the craziest things
at the Mardi Gras

I saw a man
wearing a padded bra

Running through the crowd
chasing a man in the raw

But the one thing
that got my ooh and aah

Was when a blind man
picked up a hammer and saw

SOUNDS GOOD TO ME

If lawyers are disbarred
    and clergy men are defrocked

Are models deposed
    and cowboys deranged

Should electricians be delighted
    and musicians be denoted

Should tree surgeons be debarked
    and dry cleaner be depressed

All I can say is "C'est la vie,"
    it makes sense to me.

Cotter Barry

REFLECTION

After reflection
    on my accomplishments,
        which were too few,
I suffer from regrets
    over things I didn't do.

After reflection
    on my failures,
        which would flip one's lid,
I suffer remorse
    over things I did.

CHAPTER VII

From The Land Of The Forgotten

••

Did you know that two thirds of prisoners will return to prison after they are released? After retirement, I became involved in a non- profit organization whose goal is to reduce the amount of repeats by teaching a decision making program to interested inmates. Not all prisoners want to change for to quote Philippians 3:19, "Their destiny is destruction, their god is their stomach, and their glory is in their shame."

The program is geared to show the inmates that their actions have long term consequences and they have to be responsible for their actions. A concept that seems to be absent in alot of people's lives both in and out of prison.

Scary numbers frame this issue. Seventy percent of children of incarcerated parents end up in jail themselves. About 40,000 kids in Philadelphia and 2.4 millions across our country have parents behind bars.

No doubt they are unaware of where they are heading, for the devil never tells us our destination, as he leads us along his path. To you in strife, I give my heart in rhyme.

TO THOSE IN STRIFE

Today I will know that peace is a child of justice.
    and more than the absence of war.
Today I will plant a seed of justice,
    in this my city, to grow for evermore.

Today I will love my enemies and try
    to see our differences and their worth.
Today I will live in peace with my neighbor
    and bring peace to my patch of this earth.

Today I will remember that hope is
    the most important gift I can give away.
I will be happy and remember it is up to me
    to carry my joy to all I touch this day.

Today I will test my love for thee
    by doing one act for peace and one act for life.
Today I will disarm myself by extending
    my hand in help and forgiveness to those of strife.

Cotter Barry

THE DOORS OPENED

The door opened
and in walked hope.
At that very moment
destiny spoke.

The door opened
blowing in a wind
of comforting
thoughts from a friend.

The door opened
what a surprise.
I've waited so long
for you to arrive.

The end of my loneliness,
my angst, my sorrow.
The door opened
and in came tomorrow.

LONGING

From these walls
    I want to fleece
Looking for help
    and longing for peace

Looking for light
    I wait in darkness
Looking for hope
    I'll settle for less

Wanting to correct
    the things I did wrong
Longing for forgiveness
    I yearn to belong.

Cotter Barry

MAJORITY

Because everyone
    is doing it
The wagon
    you shouldn't hitch

If the majority
    was always right
The majority
    would be rich.

CAN DO

I've learned that
    your "I can do"
is more important
    than your "IQ"

DAYDREAMS

Dream good dreams for yourself
  but more important, follow through.

Do what you need to do
  to make them come true.

SEEK HEALING

When you have been done wrong
    you have the right
      to express your feelings

But that does not give
    you the right
      to hit the ceiling

Nor does it give
    you the right
      for dirty dealing

When you are hurt
    you will find
      it much more appealing

To seek justice and
    the protection of rights
      by seeking healing

LISTEN

Listen
to the enemies
you make.

Listen
there is too much
at stake.

For they
say as much
about you,

As your
allies
so do.

THE RUN

Before reaching the sitting
    of the sun.
The twilight hour
    of a long run

You should try to learn
    before you die
What you're running from
    and why

Cotter Barry

HE UNDERSTANDS

Left behind in the shadows of gloom,
to slowly die in a windowless room.

Inside these walls, it's hard to cope
leaving one sad and without hope.

Feeling hopeless, I must confess,
I cry out to release the stress.

Like a soft whisper blowing in the wind.
The door opened and in came a friend.

Bandaging me as I bled.
He listened to all my needs.

Together, we will get over your fears.
Together, we will get through the tears.

The past can't change, said he.
Understanding the now is the key.

This lost soul, with a number for a name,
found someone who understands his pain.

PLEASE DON'T LEAVE ME

I know it was never in your plan,
that prison would be where I'd become a man.

Here, in the land of the forgotten, things occur.
Drugs, alcohol and from there, it's all a blur.

You were so proud of your first born boy.
The apple of your eye, a bundle of joy.

Who am I? What went wrong?
Was I too weak? Was I too strong?

I ask myself these questions every day.
I look in the mirror but have nothing to say.

Deep down Dad, you and I know
today I am at a long time low.

So please do not leave me, not tonight.
Give me a second chance to get it right.

Cotter Barry

A MOTHER'S PRAYER

Is this the boy I raised
    what is he doing in jail
Is this the son I loved
    he looks so frail

What has my son done
    has he caused you pain
when you arrested him
    did he call my name

Is this what you want
    is this the way you must go
Are you the boy I raised
    are you the son I used to know

I'd gladly trade places
    if I could save you some pain
But I can see the boy I raised
    and you are not the same

Tell me you are the boy I raised
    and the son I knew
For if you are the one I've loved
    I'll be able to love you too

THE PAIN BEYOND THE WALLS

I want to help him
  but I don't know how
He won't look at me
  his head is held a bow.

You didn't listen to me
  you listen to the street
Now the only time I can forget
  is when I am asleep

You had to get involved
  in drugs and alcohol
Now your suffering and pain
  is felt beyond this wall.

I fought for your life
  you fought with a fist of rage
Then came those headlines
  and your face on the front page

Now all I can do
  is sit home and wait
Until the day twelve strangers
  decide your fait

And blame myself for your
  failures and shortfalls
and silently endure
  the pain beyond the walls

Cotter Barry

CHAPTER VIII

The Golden Years

• •

For the first time in my life, I am the person I have always wanted to be. Oh not my body for that is depressing. The wrinkles, the baggy eyes, the sagging butt and those aches and pains. I'm often taken back by the old person that lives in my mirror who by the way looks like my dad. Like my Dad, when asked how I feel I found the best answer is "I'm fine."

I'm also a very thankful guy. To start, I was very fortunate to have amazing friends, a loving wife, a great son and super grandchildren. With all this going for me how can I not be thankful for a wonderful life.

At this stage of my life I have become more kind and less critical to myself. I try to eat healthy and take care of myself. However, I don't chide myself for eating the extra piece of pie! After all, I'm entitled to overeat now and then. I have seen too many dear friends leave this world too soon, before they understood the great freedom that comes with aging.

I will sing along with and even dance, by myself, to those wonderful times of the 40's and 50's and if I, in hearing a song, wish to weep over a lost friend, I will.

I know I am at times forgetful. But the way I see it, some things are best forgotten. Eventually I will remember the important things.

Over the years my heart has been broken many times. How can your heart not break when you lose a friend or a loved one. How can your heart not break when you watch a child suffer or when a pet gets hit by a car. Yet it is broken hearts that give us strength, understanding, and compassion. for a heart that was never broken will remain sterile and will never know the joy of being imperfect.

I am so blessed to have lived long enough to have my hair turn gray, to see my grandchildren and to have my youthful laughs be forever etched into deep grooves on my weather beaten face.

As you get older, it becomes easier to be positive. I care less about what other people think. I don't question myself anymore. I figure I earned the right to be wrong. As strange as it may seem, I like being old for it has set me free. I like the person I have become.

I'M FINE

There is nothing the matter with me.
    I'm just as healthy as can be.

Have a little arthritis in both my knees
    and when I climb stairs I get a wheeze.

Can't remember where I parked my car
    or the last time I had a good cigar.

Have a hard time opening some jars,
    yet I still thank my lucky stars.

As our life tales began to unfold,
    for you and me, as we're growing old

It's far better to say "I'm fine" with a grin
    than to let them know the shape we're in.

Cotter Barry

MEMORIES

Sweet are the memories
    the faces and the years
On enchanted wings of time
    like countless falling tears

Each face a little different
    yet everyone's the same
A hundred million people
    each with a different name

FREEDOM

I would have retired
    years and years ago.
It wasn't the lack of desire
    it was the lack of dough

To hunt and fish,
    no need to justify
Fish don't care
    if you wear a tie

To build a bird house
    a better mousetrap.
In the middle of the day
    take a nap

Listen to a concert
    a walk in the park.
Cocktails at pool side
    some Cutty Sark

Return to nature
    a song to be heard.
Take off to Florida
    become a snowbird

See an afternoon movie,
    read a book.
Wear shorts,
    learn how to cook

Cotter Barry

Freedom to do
    whatever you wishin
As long as you get
    your wife's permission

CHECK IT OUT

As I get old and feeble
    I found a better way
to cope with the raising cost
    for nursing home today

It has a swimming pool, a workout room,
    and a lounge, all I could hope.
Plus give me free toothpaste,
    razors, shampoo, and soap.

The senior bus and the church bus
    will charge me no fare.
For a change of lunch, take the airport bus
    and eat at the café there.

They have 24 hour service
    should I fall to the floor
There's always someone to pick me up
    what more can you ask for.

So when I reach the golden age
    help me keep my grin
and check my old rickety butt
    into the nearest Holiday Inn.

LIVE UNTIL YOU DIE

With a non functioning brain
that strains to keep out of the rain

and a will that's weak and small
so I grow wide instead of tall.

I prone to swear and stew
about things I can not do

about the times I didn't bet
and the raise I didn't get.

Yet, if I really really try
I'll surely live until I die.

CLUELESS

I wanted my wife
    to have a special day
so asked what she'd like
    for her birthday.

I'd love to be six again
    she replied in a lark.
On the morn of her birthday
    I took her to the park.

We're going to ride
    on every ride
The screaming Loop
    the Death Slide.

The Hall of Fear
    the earth Quake.
Order hot dogs
    a refreshing shake.

Five hours later
    stomache upside down.
Dinner at Burger King
    the wearing of a crown.

Staggering home
    collapsing into bed,
What was it like
    to be six again, I said.

Cotter Barry

Even when you're listening
    you still don't get it!
I meant my dress size,
    you idiot!

The moral of the story
    the singing of the song
Even when I'm listening
    I'm gonna get it all wrong.

JOURNEY

I have always dreaded getting old
 it always made me sad.
Until I got there and decided
 it really isn't that bad.

I know I can't be young again
 that doesn't take a sleuth.
I can however wander there
 and recall the joy of youth.

As well as my journey
 and the things I did with pride
Now I loudly proclaim
 that was one hell-of-a-ride.

WRINKLES

The spirit
    so I am told
will never
    grow old

If the wrinkles
    that you call art

are not written
    upon the heart

THE (SENIOR) CAT IN
THE (PLAID) HAT

I can not see.
I can not pee.

I can not hear.
Memory not clear.

My body's drooping.
have trouble pooping.

I can not sleep.
Walk at a creep.

I can not smell.
I look like _____.

I can not chew.
What can I do?

I became my dad
in my hat of plaid.

SING A SONG

Now don't forget,
    when things go wrong,
to try the magic
    of a song.

For a cheerful heart
    and a smiling face
will bring sunshine
    to the darkest place.

OPPORTUNITY

At my age
I never pass up
the chance
to get a kiss.

Opportunities
are never lost
someone will take
the one you miss.

Cotter Barry

GOLDEN YEARS

The golden years
    are here at last.
Looking back
    they got here fast.

It's not the time
    to stick one's neck out.
Just lay back and enjoy
    what's retirement about.

The golden years
    are give and take
and preparation
    for the pearly gate.

It's about being active
    and having some fun
It's about life's race
    and your final run.

The golden years
    are the last college try
working through pain
    there's no time to cry.

It's about being alone
    the last to die.
It's about burying old friends
    and saying good-bye.

The golden years
    is not about gold
It's all about
    growing old.

FLAME

The fire of my first love
    will always burn.
Down deep within, I will
    forever yearn.

I still remember,
    my old flame,
every passionate detail
    except her name.

CHAPTER IX

Farewell

••••••••••••••••••••••••••••••••••••

My parents taught me to value ordinary things like; autumn leaves, rainbows, morning dew, sun sets, summer nights, cool breezes, snow flakes, faithful pets, and friendships.

During my four years of high school I hung around constantly with four guys; Chuck, Ebs, Jack, and Rip.. During college the five of us would get together as often as we could and continued to do such until those wedding bells started breaking up that old gang of mine.

Chuck was the first to get married, followed by Rip, Ebs, myself and Jack. I always said Jack got married because he had no one to pal with. I was the best man at all four weddings. At the time, I couldn't tell you why I was the guy, however, looking back I guess I was the common link that kept the five of us connected.

When I got married, my choice for the best man was Jack because of longevity. Jack and I were friends since kindergarten. Chuck and I became friends in grade school an Rip and Ebs were picked up in high school.

For over 50 years (63 years for Jack) our friendship continued, through the good times and the bad. We enjoyed the sunny days together and rode the storms together. All these years, we never forgot where we came from. If you never forget where you came from, it will serve you well for the rest of your life.

When the Grim Reaper started knocking at our doors, we walked into the valley of the shadow of death together. Chuck was the first to be taken, followed by Rip then Jack, all yielding to cancer. A victim of Alzheimer, Ebs' body didn't leave us until January 2009. However, for years, when you looked into his hollow eyes you knew he was no longer.

A faith worse than death. Alzheimer's disease casts such a long dark shadow on families.

Death still remains a mystery to me. It is hard to imagine a world without Chuck, Rip, Jack, and Ebs. I don't know how nor do I know why I have survived all my old friends and heroes.

To quote Simon Wiesenthal (1908-2005), a survivor of a dozen Nazi Camps, who helped bring over 1,000 Nazi war criminals to justice. "Survival is a privilege which entails obligations."

As I sit here, listening to comforting soft music and sipping some good malt scotch, I start missing lost friends and those times of whispering, laughing and even crying.

The times have rushed by as did my, old friends. Someday this evening will be just a memory. But this is the present moment. I should live it as I did the lessons of the past and the dreams of the future.

I don't know how long I am going to live, but I still think of my life as an adventure. When every day is the same, it's because people fail to recognize the good things that happen in their lives every day.

Perhaps none of this matters anymore for I have already seen many people come and go. I have seen kings and servants, leaders and beggars, young and old, and the people from the land of the forgotten.

Yet in my heart, I know there is someone to whom I am to teach some of my secrets. I do not know this person yet, but I will recognize this person when he or she appears.

MISSING

I miss Chuck,
    my old grade school pal,
and the times
    we dated the same gal.

The fishing pond
    where we would skinny-dip
and our fifty years
    of friendship.

I miss Jack,
    my old drinking buddy
and the times when
    life was not so muddy.

Has anyone seen
    my old buddy Jack.
It would be so nice
    to have him back.

I miss Rip,
    my old high school friend.
those were the times
    we thought would never end.

Has anyone seen
    my old comrade Rip.
I sure miss him
    and his friendship.

Cotter Barry

I miss my buddy Ebs
    who everyone called Brin
He was a loyal
    and lasting friend.

A long friendship that
    was never lukewarm
He was there on a sunny day
    and there to ride out the storm.

I miss a lot
    now that I'm silvertip,
my old friends
    and our life trip.

Yet, I know someday
    it will again be
my old pals
    Chuck, Jack, Rip, Ebs, and me.

NOTHING

That which man loves,
    more than life,
hates more than death
    or mortal strife.

It's that which
    contended men desire,
the poor posses and
    the rich require.

It's what the miser spends
    the spend thrift saves
It's what all men carry
    to their graves.

Cotter Barry

TO SLEEP

I'm at the end of my journey
    I have sown and now I reap.
I have no more travels
    for these old legs do creep.

A silent hush breeze
    brings on the cold night air.
So read to me again
    the children's evening prayer.

It's time to prepare
    to take the quantum leap.
So read to me once more,
    now I lay down to sleep.

EULOGY

Just wing it you say
    but wouldn't it be better
To record the eulogy
    or write a letter.

That gives tribute
    where homage is due
And the opportunity
    to the remaining few.

To bring back
    the yesteryears
At a time
    long past today's tears.

Cotter Barry

AT THE GATE

I remember the day we went on our very first date.
  That was the time he was waiting at the gate.

We were in high school sharing a dream.
  That was the time he was captain of the team.

Then came the time he went to war.
  That was the time I saw him no more.

I remember the day the letter came.
  That was the time he talked about pain.

And the fear he had about going to die.
  That was the time, he said good bye.

The coffin was draped with stars and stripes.
  That was the time, for the wailing of the pipes.

Last night he told me, my old soul mate,
  it is time and he'll be waiting at the gate.

IT SEEMS LIKE ONLY YESTERDAY

It seems like only yesterday
    you went away
That was the day, I told myself
    you would be okay.

It seems like only yesterday
    you fought to stay another day.
That was the day, I knew
    you could no longer stay.

It seems like only yesterday
    I watched your smile get dim.
That was the day, I prayed
    so much more to Him.

It seems like only yesterday
    I knew it was your time.
That was the day I had to let go
    and give you peace of mind.

It seems like only yesterday
    on a cold winter night
A void was made in my heart
    that will never again see light.

Cotter Barry

HEAVEN

He shall wipe away every tear.
    There shall no longer be any fear.

There shall no longer be any crying.
    There shall no longer be any dying.

There shall no longer be any pain
    His touch will bring happiness again.

THE SPLENDOR OF HIM

Beauty will spring
    from the beast of pain
And the righteous people
    will call HIS name

They sing an ancient hymn
    of sweet and sour
The miracle of nature's splendor
    bring forth a flower

A GOOD-BYE KISS

She looked so beautiful
    sitting quietly in the chair.

Although my eyes are closed
    I see her sitting there.

Her heart speaks the kindest
    words, that anyone could say.

Although my ears can not hear
    I hear her thoughts today.

She held my hand so hard
    I thought we would never part.

Although my hands are cold
    her warmth has reached my heart.

She told me it was okay
    to leave knowing she will miss.

Although my lips are cold
    I felt her good-bye kiss.

KEEP IN TOUCH

He lights up the room
    with a smile so bright.
The center of attention
    at our poker night.

A friends to so many
    too many to name.
The love for each of them
    was his claim to fame.

Easy to talk to
    such a great friend.
Confide in him
    your problems he'll mend.

A gift from God
    how blessed were we,
to know such a man
    as strong as he.

So many memories
    I will miss him so much.
But knowing John,
    he'll keep I touch.

GOING HOME

Battling the ravages of cancer
  he went to great length.
When I looked into his eyes
  I saw courage and quiet strength.

I couldn't help noticing
  how he clinged to his faith.
He looked forward
  to going home, so he saith.

A brave soldier was he,
  as he fought the Grim Reaper.
Through his suffering
  his faith grew deeper.

He told me not to grieve
  for he loved me still.
Look beyond earth's shadows
  and trust our Father's will.

All his pain and grief is over,
  his restless days have passed.
He is now at peace forever
  safely home in Heaven at last.

The wailing of bagpipes
  set the pace.
With the mournful rasp
  of Amazing Grace.

The sound of the thunder
    surrounded us from the sky
As a squadron of fighters
    honored him with a flyby.

They covered him with a flag
    like thatching,
As sadden faces
    and hollow eyes sat watching.

I will miss my friend
    yet I feel blessed
for his suffering is over
    and he is home at rest.

Cotter Barry

IT AIN'T ME

So you think I look cute
All decked out in this monkey suit

Let me tell you, it ain't me
the guy you think you see

Many years went silently
They were good times, you'll have to agree

The grey haired geezer, looking up at thee
Let me tell you, it ain't me

Always together all those years.
Please for me wipe away your tears

Open your heart and listen to my plea.
The guy you're looking at, it ain't me

MY MYSTERY

Has anyone noticed, the quiet dignity
once found on my face, is now history

What's left for me, my goodbyes are said
What isn't written, will remain my mystery

www.ingramcontent.com/pod-product-compliance
Lightning Source LLC
Chambersburg PA
CBHW032015170526
45157CB00002B/701